TikTok Cookbook for Influencers

Legal Notice

Copyright 2022 Zara London

The author offers information only.

No advice, health, legal, or otherwise, is offered in this book.

All rights are reserved.

TikTok Cookbook for Influencers

Delicious Meals and Extravagant Treats to go Viral

Zara London

Contents

Breakfast Any Time

Pesto Egg-In-A-Hole

Serves: 1 / Preparation time: 5 minutes / Cooking time: 5 minutes

1 tablespoon pesto, store-bought or homemade

Freshly ground black pepper

1 slice of bread, such as ciabatta or sourdough

Kosher salt

1 large egg

- Place a slice of bread onto a flat surface and cut an egg-sized hole using a paring knife or a cup.

- Preheat pesto in a small-sized nonstick pan.

- Place bread and bread cut-out in the pan, then crack an egg into the bread hole.

- Cook for a couple of minutes, then flip over and cook for another minute or two.

- Once done, transfer to a serving platter and season with pepper and salt to your liking.

Yogurt Toast

Serves: 1 / Preparation time: 2 minutes / Cooking time: 15 minutes

1/4 cup Greek yogurt

Pinch of cinnamon

2 thick slices of bread such as brioche, wheat, or sourdough

2 tablespoons maple syrup, agave, honey, or melted chocolate, plus more for drizzling

1 large egg

Topping:

Strawberries

Raspberries

Blueberries

Optional Servings:

Toasted oats

Chocolate shavings

Powdered sugar

Dried coconut

- Preheat the oven to 400°F.

- Add maple syrup, cinnamon, yogurt, and egg to a medium-sized bowl and whisk well.

- Press the back of a spoon or your fingers into the center of the bread slice to create a well without tearing. Then fill it with the prepared custard mixture.

- Do the same with another bread slice.

- Place berry or a mix of berries on top of the custard.

- Place bread slices on a baking sheet and bake in a preheated oven for 10 to 13 minutes until golden brown.

- Once done, take it out of the oven and transfer it to a serving platter.

- Serve immediately topped with your favorite toppings.

Japanese Soufflé Pancakes

Serves: 2 / Preparation time: 20 minutes / Cooking time: 25 minutes

3 large egg whites

Agave or maple syrup

2 large egg yolks

Softened butter

2 tablespoons milk

2 tablespoons water

1/2 teaspoon almond extract

Neutral oil (for greasing)

1 lemon, zested

3 1/2 tablespoons powdered sugar

1/4 cup all-purpose flour, sifted

1/2 teaspoon lemon juice

1/4 teaspoon kosher salt

1/4 teaspoon cream of tartar

- Combine milk, lemon zest, egg yolks, almond extract, and milk in a medium-sized bowl.

- Next, whisk in the salt and flour until smooth. Set the bowl aside.

- Whisk lemon juice and egg whites together in a stand mixer with a whisk attachment. Beat well until frothy.

- Then add in the cream of tartar while whisking.

- Once everything is incorporated, add powdered sugar and continue whipping on medium-high speed until it reaches a stiff peak. It may take around 8 to 10 minutes. The meringue must resemble the texture of a marshmallow.

- Grease 4 ring molds and place them in a large nonstick skillet over low flame.

- Lightly grease the pan with a neutral oil, wiping away the excess oil. Turn on the flame to medium and let the pan preheat.

- Combine egg yolk base and 1/3 of the meringue until incorporated.

- Gently fold in the remaining meringue until no more steaks are visible.

- Now create 4 even mounds by scooping the batter into prepared ring molds. Do not overfill the ring.

- Fill the pan with a tablespoon of water and cover it with the lid.

- Cook the pancakes for about 8 minutes until the bottoms have turned golden brown.

- Then flip over the pancakes carefully in their rings and add another tablespoon of water to a pan. Put on the lid and cook for another 5 to 6 minutes.

- Once done, remove the ring mold using a pair of silicone tongs.

- Trim the extra sides of the pancakes with a butter knife.

- Enjoy delicious pancakes topped with agave and softened butter!

Blended Baked Oats

Serves: 1 / Preparation time: 5 minutes / Cooking time: 25 minutes

1 large egg	1/2 cup rolled old-fashioned oats
2 tablespoons Nutella	1 tablespoon maple syrup
Cooking spray	2 bananas, divided
3/4 teaspoon baking powder	1/2 cup of milk of choice

- Preheat the oven to 350°F.
- Grind oats in a blender until you have a fine powder, and keep it aside.
- Mash one banana in a medium-sized bowl until smooth.
- Whisk in the milk, egg, and maple syrup until incorporated.
- Next, gently fold in baking powder and ground oats until it turns into a pourable batter.
- Pour batter into a greased baking dish, followed by dollops of Nutella in different spots.
- Swirl Nutella through the batter using a butter knife.
- Top the batter with the remaining slices of banana.
- Bake for about 25 minutes, or until the tester inserted comes out clean from the center.
- Serve and enjoy

Rebel Within Muffins

Serves: 9 / Preparation time: 10 minutes / Cooking time: 20 minutes

1 teaspoon kosher salt

1/4 cup sliced chives

11 large eggs, divided

1 cup shredded cheddar, divided

Cooking spray

1 tablespoon maple syrup

2 1/2 cups all-purpose flour

1/2 cup sour cream

1 tablespoon baking powder

1 cup (2 sticks) butter, melted

- Fill a pot with an inch of water and place 9 eggs into it. Turn on the flame and bring to a boil, covered. Then turn off the flame and let the eggs sit for 4 to 5 minutes, covered.

- In the meantime, prepare an ice bath by adding 2 cups of ice and water to a large bowl.

- Place eggs in the ice bath and let them sit for 3 minutes. Then peel the eggs and place them in the refrigerator.

- Preheat the oven to 400°F.

- Take a muffin tin and grease it with cooking spray, including the tops of the pan.

- Combine baking powder, flour, and salt in a medium-sized bowl.

- In a separate bowl, whisk together sour cream, remaining 2 eggs, butter, and maple syrup.

- Stir in the dry ingredients and then fold in all the chives and 2/3 cup of cheddar. The batter should resemble cookie dough.

- Now fill each muffin cup with 2 tablespoons of the prepared batter and press it about halfway up the sides using your fingers. Top each with 1 soft-boiled egg, covering each egg with more batter. Once eggs are coated with the batter on all sides, top them with remaining cheddar.

- Bake in a preheated oven for about 15 to 18 minutes, until golden brown.

- Enjoy as is or chilled!

Smashed Brussels Sprouts

Serves: 6-8 / Preparation time: 10 minutes / Cooking time: 40 minutes

1 teaspoon freshly chopped thyme

Freshly chopped parsley, for garnish

2 lbs. Brussels sprouts

1/4 cup freshly grated Parmesan

2 tablespoons extra-virgin olive oil

1 cup shredded mozzarella

2 cloves garlic, minced

Freshly ground black pepper

Kosher salt

- Preheat the oven to 425°F.

- Meanwhile, prepare an ice bath in a large-sized bowl and line a baking sheet with parchment paper.

- Add Brussels to a pot with salted water and bring to a boil. Cook for about 8 to 10 minutes, until tender. Then transfer them to an ice bath. Drain well.

- Transfer blanched Brussels to a parchment-lined baking sheet and toss with garlic, oil, and thyme.

- Smash Brussels sprouts into a flat patty using the end of a small glass.

- Season the sprouts with pepper and salt, followed by Parmesan and mozzarella on top.

- Bake in a preheated oven for about 20 to 25 minutes, until crispy and golden.

- Serve garnished with fresh parsley!

Blueberry Baked Oats (Vegan)

Serves: 2 / Preparation time: 6 minutes / Cooking time: 30 minutes

1 cup of almond milk

⅓ cup frozen blueberries

1 cup of rolled oats

2 tablespoons maple syrup

1 ripe banana

1 teaspoon chai spice (or ground cinnamon)

1 teaspoon of baking powder

- Preheat the oven to 375 °F.

- Add banana, maple syrup, oats, chai spice, baking powder, and milk to a blender and blitz to combine until oats have broken down, for 30 seconds to a minute.

- Divide the mixture between two ramekins (10 oz. each) and top with blueberries.

- Bake for half an hour.

- Remove from oven and enjoy!

Ramen With Milk

Serves: 1 / Preparation time: 4 minutes / Cooking time: 8 minutes

1 egg

1 teaspoon chili oil (optional)

1 package of instant ramen

2 chopped green onion

1 cup of milk

- Cook noodles as per the instructions mentioned in the package. Drain well.

- Bring milk to a boil and stir in the sauce packet. Add noodles, stir well, and then turn the heat to medium.

- Create a well in the noodles and crack an egg into it, followed by a sprinkle of chopped green onions. Cook for 2 minutes, and then turn off the flame.

- Scoop up the poached egg using a spoon and transfer milk and noodles into a bowl.

- Top with the egg and sprinkle with sesame seeds.

- Finish off with a drizzle of chill oil and serve right away!

Nature's Cereal Recipe

Serves: 1 / Preparation time: 5 minutes / Cooking time: 0 minutes

¼ cup pomegranate seeds

½ cup ice

1 cup blueberries

1 tablespoon chopped fresh mint

1 cup raspberries

1 cup coconut water

1 cup blackberries

- Add all the ingredients to a bowl and mix well.

- Serve as it or chilled!

Chili Oil Eggs

Serves: 2 / Preparation time: 2 minutes / Cooking time: 5 minutes

2 cups cooked rice

Pinch of white and black sesame seeds

2 tablespoons chili oil

Pinch of sea salt

2 eggs

2 teaspoons furikake seasoning

- Spread chili oil in a nonstick frying pan and let it preheat over medium flame.

- Crack eggs into the pan and cook for 2 minutes while pouring some oil on top of the eggs using a spoon.

- Cover the pan and cook until egg whites are no longer translucent.

- Divide rice between the serving bowls and sprinkle each with a teaspoon of furikake.

- Place one egg in each and pour the leftover oil from the pan over each egg.

- Finish off with a sprinkle of sesame seeds and sea salt.

Grated Egg Avocado Toast

Serves: 1 / Preparation time: 6 minutes / Cooking time: 15 minutes

2 cups loosely packed kale leaves

2 cups liquid egg whites, beaten

1 cup chopped broccoli

1 large white onion, julienned

1 large red sweet pepper, julienned

1 teaspoon garlic powder

Salt and ground black pepper, to taste

2 teaspoons ghee

- Spread mayonnaise over a slice of bread.

- Place avocado in the center of the bread and spread it to the edges using a spoon.

- Scatter hardboiled eggs onto the avocado and sprinkle with pepper and salt to your liking.

- Spread microgreens across the top and enjoy immediately.

Chocolate Baked Oats

Serves: 2 / Preparation time: 5 minutes / Cooking time: 30 minutes

1 teaspoon baking powder

2 tablespoons dark chocolate chunks (or chips)

1 cup rolled oats

2 tablespoons honey

¾ cup almond milk

¼ teaspoon kosher salt

1 egg

2¼ teaspoon kosher salt

1 very ripe banana

2 teaspoons cocoa powder

- Preheat the oven to 375 °F.

- Blend baking powder, oats, cocoa powder, banana, almond milk, egg, salt, and honey in a blender until oats are broken down for a minute.

- Divide the oat mixture between two ramekins and top each with chocolate chunks.

- Bake in a preheated oven for half an hour.

- Serve and enjoy!

Breakfast Casserole

Serves: 8 / Preparation time: 10 minutes / Cooking time: 50 minutes

Pepper to taste

8 eggs

1 can 8-count jumbo biscuits

2 cups Mexican-style shredded cheese

1 16 oz. pork sausage roll

1 cup milk

1 teaspoon salt

- Preheat the oven to 350 °F.

- Brown sausage in a skillet until fully cooked, for about 10 minutes. Set aside.

- Whisk milk, eggs, pepper, and salt in a bowl.

- Press the biscuits into a baking dish (9x13) until the entire space is covered. Do not overlap the biscuits.

- Add sausage, beaten eggs, and cheese, and bake for half an hour, uncovered.

- Add the browned sausage

- Add the beaten eggs

- Cover the dish with foil and continue baking for another 20 minutes.

- Once done, take them out of the oven and let them cool before slicing.

Easy Caramel Apple Wrap

Serves: 3 / Preparation time: 10 minutes / Cooking time: 5 minutes

1 tablespoon unsalted butter

Caramel sauce

1 Granny Smith apple, sliced

3 large tortillas

½ cup packed brown sugar

½ cup granulated sugar

2 teaspoon vanilla extract

- Place granulated sugar, brown sugar, vanilla extract, and butter in a heavy-bottom saucepan and cook until bubbling.

- Then stir in the sliced apples and cook for a minute or two. Turn off the flame.

- Now start folding the tortilla first in half, then in half again to create 4 equal quadrants, then unfold.

- Now create a slit at the halfway mark from middle to edge to create a single slit.

- Take 2 quadrants and place apple slices into them.

- Take another 2 quadrants and spread caramel sauce onto them.

- Carefully fold over the tortilla and then fold it to the side, covering the other sauce mixture.

- Then seal it into a triangle with a final fold.

- Repeat the same for all the tortillas.

- Place tortilla in a preheated skillet and cook until toasted on both sides. Flip over and cook for another 2 minutes.

- Add additional butter if needed.

- Enjoy with sauce, caramelized apples, and whipped cream.

Tiktok Egg Vegetable Sandwich

Serves: 1 / Preparation time: 5 minutes / Cooking time: 10 minutes

1 teaspoon milk

1 tablespoon carrots, tiny chopped

1 teaspoon butter

1 tablespoon Zucchini, tiny chopped

2 large pieces of sandwich bread

2-3 tablespoons cheese, shredded

2 eggs, beaten

2 slices bacon, cooked and torn into pieces

Salt and pepper, to taste

- Combine milk, eggs, salt, and pepper in a medium-sized bowl.

- Preheat butter in a skillet over medium flame.

- Once hot, pour the egg mixture into the skillet and place two bread slices on top right next to each other.

- Flip over the bread carefully so both sides get coated with the egg mixture.

- Once the bottom has cooked, flip over and top with bacon, sautéed onion, and cheese.

- Fold edges onto the bread carefully, flipping one bread piece over another to create a sandwich.

- Remove the sandwich and cut it in half before serving.

Tiktok Viral Breakfast Quesadilla

Serves: 2 / Preparation time: 10 minutes / Cooking time: 8 minutes

1 tomato, sliced into roughly 3/4–inch slices

Chopped parsley for garnish

2 large eggs, room temperature

1/4 avocado, sliced

Fine salt, to taste

2 large lettuce leaves

Freshly ground black pepper, to taste

3 tablespoons grated cheese mix

1 teaspoon butter

1 tortilla

1/2 red onion, sliced

- Beat 2 eggs in a medium-sized bowl and then season with pepper and salt to your liking. Whisk again until no lump is there.

- Preheat butter in a pan over medium flame.

- Place onion and tomato slices in a pan and let them cook for 3 to 5 minutes. Then flip over and cook another side for 2 to 3 minutes.

- Next, add the egg mixture to the pan and let it cook for 4 to 5 minutes.

- Place tortilla on top of the egg mixture and cook until cooked through, for a minute or two.

- Gently flip over the omelet and turn off the flame. Let it sit for 2 to 3 minutes.

- Scatter the top with grated cheese, followed by lettuce leaves and avocado slices.

- Now fold the tortilla and enjoy it immediately, garnished with chopped parsley.

Viral Bella Hadid Sandwich

Serves: 1 / Preparation time: 10 minutes / Cooking time: 0 minutes

For Dressing:

1 teaspoon dried oregano

A few pinches of salt

1 tablespoon olive oil

A few pinches of ground black pepper

1 tablespoon balsamic vinegar

1 teaspoon dried red chili flakes

1 teaspoon dried basil

For Basil Aioli:

2 tablespoons freshly chopped basil

3 tablespoons mayonnaise

½ tablespoon Dijon mustard

For Salad:

2 cups lettuce, shredded

1 teaspoon red wine vinegar

½ red onion, minced

½ tablespoon lemon juice

For Assembling:

2 to 3 cooked turkey breast slices

2 tomatoes, sliced

Italian bread or sub buns

3 slices of provolone cheese

3 pepperoncini peppers, pickled, sliced

5 salami slices, round cut

- Combine all the dressing ingredients in a bowl and refrigerate until ready to use.

- Take another bowl and combine the basil aioli ingredients. Place it in the refrigerator, too.

- Combine lettuce and red onions in a large-sized bowl. Toss with red wine vinegar and lemon juice.

- Add prepared dressing and toss well, reserving ½ tablespoon for later use.

- To assemble, half the sub bun or Italian bread and spread one of the slices with slices of pepperoncini pepper.

- Spread the prepared salad over the peppers, followed by a few salami slices, provolone cheese slices, 2 tomato slices, and a few pinches of salt.

- Drizzle with the preserved dressing.

- Smear another slice of bread with basil aioli and top with turkey slices.

- Gently fold the slices of bread to create a sandwich.

- Serve and enjoy!

TikTok Bacon & Cheese Sandwich

Serves: 1 / Preparation time: 10 minutes / Cooking time: 5 minutes

2 slices bread

2 slices bacon, cooked and crumbled

1 tablespoon butter

1/4 cup cheese, shredded

2 eggs, beaten

- Crack eggs into a bowl and beat well. Then pour over the butter and cover with 2 slices of bread.

- Carefully flip over, folding the overlapping egg onto bread pieces.

- Scatter bacon and cheese over the egg and cook for a minute.

- Enjoy a delicious bacon cheese sandwich for your breakfast!

Air Fryer Breakfast Cookie

Serves: 2-3 / Preparation time: 5 minutes / Cooking time: 8 minutes

1 tablespoon melted coconut oil

1 tablespoon mini chocolate chips

½ cup old-fashioned oats

Sprinkle of ground cinnamon

½ cup ripe banana

1 tablespoon milk

½ teaspoon baking powder

- Combine ripe bananas and oats in a bowl and mash them together using a fork.
- Whisk in the melted coconut oil, baking powder, and milk.
- Add mini chocolate chips and ground cinnamon and continue mixing.
- Line the air fryer basket with parchment paper and pour batter into it, spreading it to about 1/2" thick and 4" in diameter.
- Set the Air Fryer to 375°F for 8 minutes.
- Once the cooking cycle is complete, remove the cookie and let it cool before serving.

TikTok's Inside Out Omelets

Serves: 2 / Preparation time: 5 minutes / Cooking time: 10 minutes

Salt and pepper to taste

Avocado slices and grilled tomato to serve

2 eggs

Thyme or herbs of your choice

2 tablespoons pure cream

¼ cup grated cheese

- Whisk eggs, cream, pepper, and salt in a medium-sized bowl.
- Preheat a nonstick skillet over medium flame and then sprinkle cheese over the surface evenly.
- Once the cheese has melted, pour the egg-cream mixture into the skillet, tilting it to spread evenly.
- Cook until done.
- Sprinkle the omelet with herbs and then fold it in half.
- Enjoy with grilled tomato and avocado.

Perfect Party Plates

Sesame Peanut Noodles

Serves: 4 / Preparation time: 10 minutes / Cooking time: 0 minutes

1 clove garlic

Scallion, sliced, for garnish

½ cup peanut butter

¾ cup edamame shelled

3 tablespoons low-sodium soy sauce

½ cup shredded carrot

2 tablespoons sesame oil

1 tablespoon black sesame seeds for garnish

2 tablespoons rice vinegar

Peanut, for garnish

3 tablespoons water

½ cup shredded red cabbage

2 ½ teaspoons brown sugar

8 oz. spaghetti, cooked according to package instructions

½ tablespoon fresh ginger, minced

- Add soy sauce, peanut butter, water, rice vinegar, sesame oil, garlic, brown sugar, and ginger to a blender and blitz to combine until smooth.

- Add spaghetti, cabbage, carrots, and edamame to a medium-sized bowl and top with the peanut sauce. Toss well until evenly coated.

- Transfer to serving bowls and top with black sesame seeds, peanuts, and scallion.

Grinder Salad Sandwich

Serves: 4 / Preparation time: 10 minutes / Cooking time: 20 minutes

1 1/2 teaspoons dried oregano

1/2 cup sliced banana peppers

1 loaf of bread, such as Italian, ciabatta, or focaccia

1/2 cup giardiniera, roughly chopped

4 oz. provolone and/or fontina cheese, thinly sliced

1/2 medium white onion, thinly sliced

4 oz. ham, thinly sliced

1 small head of iceberg lettuce, thinly sliced

8 oz. cured Italian meat

1/4 teaspoon sugar

3/4 cup mayonnaise

1/4 teaspoon red pepper flakes

2 cloves garlic, grated or minced

1/2 teaspoon freshly ground black pepper

2 tablespoons red wine vinegar

1/2 teaspoon kosher salt

Thick tomato slices and freshly grated Parmesan for serving

- Preheat the oven to 375°F.

- Place a loaf onto a flat surface and slice it in half lengthwise, scooping out the insides.

- Place hollowed-out loaf halves on a sheet tray.

- Top one half of the loaf with layers of ham and cured meat, then the other with provolone and/or fontina.

- Bake in a preheated oven for 12 to 15 minutes until the cheese is melted.

- In the meantime, combine vinegar, mayonnaise, garlic, salt, oregano, red pepper flakes, black pepper, and sugar.

- Take another bowl and toss onion, banana peppers, lettuce, and giardiniera.

- Add a little dressing and toss well. You can add more dressing if desired.

- Top the meat half of the sandwich with tomatoes and Parmesan, followed by enough grinder salad. Then close it with the cheese half.

- Serve the sandwich with chips and grinder salad alongside.

Keto Cloud Bread

Serves: 8 / Preparation time: 10 minutes / Cooking time: 30 minutes

For Plain Cloud Bread:

1/4 teaspoon cream of tartar

2 oz. cream cheese softened

3 large eggs at room temperature

Pinch of kosher salt

For Pizza Cloud Bread:

1 tablespoon Italian seasoning

2 teaspoons tomato paste

2 tablespoons mozzarella or grated Parmesan, shredded

For Everything Bagel Cloud Bread:

1 teaspoon sesame seeds

1 teaspoon minced dried onion

1/8 teaspoon kosher salt

1 teaspoon minced dried garlic

1 teaspoon poppy seeds

For Ranch Cloud Bread:

1 1/2 teaspoon ranch seasoning powder

For Plain Cloud Bread:

- Preheat the oven to 300°F.

- Separate the egg whites from the yolks.

- Add salt and cream of tartar to the egg whites and then beat well using a hand mixer for a couple of minutes.

- Add cream cheese to the yolks and beat it well using a hand mixer until combined.

- Gently fold the egg yolk mixture into the egg white mixture.

- Divide the batter into 8 mounds on a parchment-lined baking sheet, spacing them about 4" apart.

- Bake in a preheated oven for 25 to 30 minutes until golden.

- Sprinkle each bread piece with cheese and bake for 2 to 3 minutes.

- Enjoy!

For Pizza Cloud Bread:

- Add a tablespoon of Italian seasoning, 2 teaspoons of tomato paste, and 2 tablespoons of grated Parmesan or shredded mozzarella.

For Everything Bagel Cloud Bread:

- Add 1 teaspoon poppy seeds, ⅛ teaspoon kosher salt, 1 teaspoon minced dried garlic, 1 teaspoon sesame seeds, and 1 teaspoon minced dried onion.

For Ranch Cloud Bread:

- Add 1½ teaspoons ranch seasoning powder to the egg yolk mixture.

Corn Ribs

Serves: 4 / Preparation time: 5 minutes / Cooking time: 25 minutes

For The Corn:

1 clove garlic, grated

1 ear corn, quartered lengthwise

1 tablespoon butter, melted

Freshly ground black pepper

1/2 teaspoon ground coriander

1/8 teaspoon cayenne pepper (optional)

1/2 teaspoon ground cumin

1/4 teaspoon brown sugar (optional)

1/2 teaspoon smoked paprika

1/4 teaspoon kosher salt

For The Dipping Sauce:

1 tablespoon lime juice

Kosher salt

1/4 cup Greek yogurt

1/2 teaspoon smoked paprika

- Preheat the oven to 375°F.

- Combine coriander, melted butter, salt, brown sugar, a few cranks of black pepper, paprika, cayenne, garlic, and cumin in a bowl.

- Brush the kernel side of the corn pieces with the prepared mix on all sides and place them on a baking sheet.

- Bake until corn is lightly curled and golden, for about 20 to 25 minutes.

- In the meantime, prepare dipping sauce by combining the ingredients mentioned in this section.

- Serve warm corn ribs with dipping sauce, and enjoy!

Berries and Cream Charcuterie Board

Serves: 8-10 / Preparation time: 20 minutes / Cooking time: 0 minutes

Sweet Whipped Ricotta:

8 oz. whole-milk ricotta cheese

Pinch of kosher salt

1 tablespoon honey

Assembly:

Homemade or store-bought angel food cake, biscuits, pound cake, or shortbread cookies

Whipped cream and mint leaves for serving

1 cup each of blueberries, strawberries, cherries, raspberries, and blackberries

Sweet Whipped Ricotta:

- Blend honey, ricotta, and salt in a blender/food processor for a minute or two, until fluffy. Transfer to a serving bowl.

Assembly:

- Cut baked goods into star shapes using a star-shaped cookie cutter.

- Rinse the fruit and pat it dry using paper towels.

- Arrange small bowls of whipped cream and ricotta on a serving platter alongside baked goods.

- Arrange fruit around the bowls and garnish with mint leaves.

- Serve and enjoy!

Hasselback Potatoes

Serves: 4 / Preparation time: 5 minutes / Cooking time: 1 hour 15 minutes

For The Hasselback Potatoes:

3 tablespoons extra-virgin olive oil

Freshly ground black pepper

4 large russet potatoes

Kosher salt

1 large clove of garlic, grated

For The Cream Cheese Sauce:

1/4 cup boiling water

4 tablespoons cream cheese, softened

For The Everything Bagel Seasoning:

1 tablespoon dried onion flakes

1 teaspoon kosher salt

1 tablespoon white sesame seeds

1 tablespoon poppy seeds

1 tablespoon black sesame seeds

1 tablespoon dried minced garlic

For Topping:

Sriracha or hot sauce (optional)

Freshly chopped chives

Diced red onions

Bake Hasselback Potatoes:

- Preheat the oven to 425°F.

- Place a potato lengthwise between two chopsticks on a cutting board.

- Partially slice each into ⅛"-thick slices.

- Place potato slices onto a large-sized baking sheet.

- Combine garlic and oil in a small-sized bowl.

- Brush the potato slices with half the garlic-oil mixture, and then season each with pepper and salt to your liking.

- Bake in a preheated oven for half an hour.

- Remove the potato slices and then gently squeeze them out while twisting them with your thumb and index finger.

- Brush the potatoes with the remaining garlic oil mixture and bake for another 40 minutes, until potatoes are tender and silvered topes turn deeply golden and crispy.

Make Cheese Sauce + Topping:

- In the meantime, whisk cream cheese and boiling water together in a small-sized bowl until smooth.

- Combine dried onion, sesame seeds, poppy seeds, and dried garlic in another bowl.

- Drizzle hot sauce and cream cheese sauce over the baked potatoes.

- Finish off with a sprinkle with everything seasoning, chives, and red onions.

TikTok Pizza Rolls

Serves: 25 rolls / Preparation time: 5 minutes / Cooking time: 15 minutes

¼ cup unsalted butter, melted

1 teaspoon Italian seasoning

25 frozen pizza rolls

1 clove garlic, finely minced

¼ cup grated parmesan cheese

- Preheat the oven as per the instructions mentioned in the package.

- Start lining the pizza rolls evenly in rows on a parchment-lined baking sheet and bake as per the directions given in the package.

- In the meantime, prepare the garlic butter mixture by combining Parmesan, butter, Italian seasoning, and garlic in a bowl.

- Once done with baking, place the pizza rolls in a large bowl and top with garlic butter. Toss well until coated on all sides.

- Serve and enjoy!

Viral Tiktok Loaded Buffalo Cheese Fries Recipe

Serves: 12 / Preparation time: 10 minutes / Cooking time: 20 minutes

1 teaspoon of onion powder

Ranch dressing (topping)

1 (32 oz.) bag of frozen french fries

4 strips of bacon, chopped

½ a cup of your favorite wing sauce

1 (32 oz.) block of Velveeta cheese (original)

1 bundle of green onion (chopped)

1 teaspoon of seasoned salt

- Preheat the oven as per the directions mentioned in the bag of frozen fries.

- Surround the cheese block with fries and pour over the wing sauce.

- Top with green onions, seasoned salt, onion powder, and bacon.

- Bake until the cheese has melted.

- Finish off with a drizzle of ranch dressing.

- Enjoy warm!

Booty Dip

Serves: 6 / Preparation time: 10 minutes / Cooking time: 0 minutes

Dippers animal crackers or vanilla wafers

4 oz. whipped topping thawed

7 oz. marshmallow fluff

12 oz. mini chocolate chips

8 oz. whipped cream cheese

1 tablespoon brown sugar

- Beat room temperature whipped cream cheese, marshmallow fluff, brown sugar, and thawed whipped topping (Cool Whip) in a large-sized bowl.

- Gently fold in mini chocolate chips until incorporated.

- Enjoy with Graham crackers, vanilla wafers, and fresh fruit of your choice.

Cheese And Bacon Butter Bath Scones

Serves: 9 / Preparation time: 20 minutes / Cooking time: 25 minutes

2 1/2 cups self-raising flour

3 shortcut bacon rashers, finely chopped

125g butter, melted

3/4 cup coarsely grated cheddar

2 cups buttermilk

- Preheat the oven to 392°F.

- Add melted butter to a square (base size) ovenproof dish.

- Add flour to a medium-sized bowl and create a well in the center.

- Gently stir in the buttermilk until well-combines.

- Place dough in the prepared dish and spread it out to the edges of the dish using the back of a spoon.

- Now cut the dough into 9 even-sized squares using an egg lifter in a downward cutting motion.

- Sprinkle the tops with bacon and cheese.

- Bake in a preheated oven for about 20 to 25 minutes, until golden.

- Once done, enjoy warm!

Micro French Onion Cob Loaves

Serves: 24 / Preparation time: 15 minutes / Cooking time: 20 minutes

2 garlic cloves, crushed

3 green shallots, thinly sliced

2 x 250g packet of fresh pizza dough at room temperature

1 tablespoon salt-reduced French onion soup mix

2 teaspoons olive oil, plus extra, to brush

1/3 cup pre-grated cheese blend

1/2 x 250g packet of frozen spinach, thawed

1/4 cup pouring cream

1 small brown onion, finely chopped

100g sour cream

125g cream cheese, at room temperature, chopped

- Take two 12-hole mini muffin pans and grease them lightly.
- Divide dough into 24 portions and roll each into a ball.
- Place a ball in each muffin pan.
- Brush the tops of the balls with extra oil.
- Bake in a preheated oven until lightly golden, for about 8 to 10 minutes.
- In the meantime, squeeze out the spinach as much as possible.
- Preheat oil in a pan and sauté garlic and onion for about 5 minutes, until softened.
- Turn the heat down and stir in the cream cheese, spinach, pure cream, sour cream, soup mix, and cheese blend until smooth.
- Turn off the flame and stir in two-thirds of the shallot.
- Season with pepper to your liking.
- Cut 1 cm top off each cob.
- Scoop out the inside of the bread, leaving a thick shell of 5mm.
- Divide the prepared spinach mixture equally among the cobs, replacing the tops.

- Turn the oven temperature down to 365°F and bake until golden brown, for about 7 to 10 minutes.

- Enjoy garnished with leftover shallots!

Pancake Shaker Impossible Quiche

Serves: 2 / Preparation time: 5 minutes / Cooking time: 45 minutes

1 cup original (plain) pancake mix

2 green shallots, thickly sliced

4 eggs, lightly whisked

2/3 cup coarsely grated cheddar

1 1/2 cups milk

100g double-smoked leg ham, coarsely chopped

50g butter, melted

1 zucchini, coarsely grated

- Preheat the oven to 392°F.

- Grease a pie dish (19cm base size).

- Whisk butter, milk, eggs, and pancake mix in a medium-sized bowl. Season the mixture to your liking.

- Squeeze out the zucchini as much as you can to remove excess water.

- Scatter cheddar, ham, shallot, and zucchini over the base of the pie dish, followed by egg mixture on top.

- Bake until golden, for about 40 to 45 minutes.

- Once done, let the quiche sit at room temperature for half an hour before serving.

Country French Potato Bake

Serves: 6 / Preparation time: 30 minutes / Cooking time: 1 hour 30 minutes

1 1/2 cups pre-grated cheddar

3/4 cup salt-reduced chicken stock

1.5kg potatoes, peeled

25g butter, finely chopped

4 garlic cloves, thinly sliced

- Preheat the oven to 392°F.

- Take a 22 x 11cm, 6 cm-deep loaf pan (base size) and line it with baking paper allowing it to overhang the long sides.

- Thinly slice the potatoes with a sharp knife or a mandolin.

- Line the side and base of the pan with potato slices, slightly overlapping in a single layer.

- Sprinkle with ½ cup of the cheese, reserving another half cup for the top.

- Top with the 2 layers of potato in an overlapped manner.

- Scatter over garlic, cheese, and butter, followed by a little stock. Season.

- Again layer with the cheese, garlic, remaining potato, and stock, seasoning between each layer, finishing with potato.

- Top with the remaining cheese.

- Now fold the overhanging baking paper and cover tightly with the foil.

- Bake in a preheated oven for an hour.

- Remove the foil and continue baking for another half an hour.

- Once done, let it cool before serving.

- Place potato bake onto a cutting board and cut into thick slices.

- Enjoy!

Air Fryer Garlic Bread Croissant Roll-Ups

Serves: 6 / Preparation time: 10 minutes / Cooking time: 10 minutes

360g pkt Coles Frozen Bake At Home Butter Croissants, slightly thawed

1 1/2 cups Coles Pizza Blend Shredded Cheese

80g garlic butter spread, softened

- Roll out the croissants using a floured rolling pin until 8mm thick.

- Top with two-thirds of the garlic butter and spread evenly.

- Then top with two-thirds of the cheese and spread again.

- Now start rolling up the croissants.

- Coat the rolls with the remaining butter until coated on all sides, and then top with the remaining cheese.

- Line your air fryer basket with baking paper and place rolls in it.

- Cook for 8 to 10 minutes at 356°F.

- Once done, remove to a serving platter and drizzle with melted garlic butter.

Custard And Golden Syrup Crumpet Tray Bake

Serves: 6 / Preparation time: 5 minutes / Cooking time: 10 minutes

6 square crumpets

¼ cup golden syrup

20g butter for greasing

11/2 cups vanilla custard

- Preheat the grill.

- Place crumpets (holes-sides down) in a greased tray and grill until lightly golden, for about 3 to 4 minutes.

- Pour over the custard evenly, followed by a drizzle of golden syrup.

- Gill for another 5 minutes and then serve immediately!

Air Fryer French Onion Potato Sticks

Serves: 16 / Preparation time: 15 minutes / Cooking time: 30 minutes

40g packet French onion soup mix

Sea salt flakes, to serve (optional)

1 cup coarsely grated mozzarella

600g Sebago (brushed) potatoes, peeled, coarsely chopped

Finely chopped fresh chives or green shallots to serve

1/2 cup cornflour

1/2 cup sour cream

- Place potatoes in a pot with cold water. Cover the pot and bring it to a boil. Then turn the heat down and simmer until potatoes are tender, for about 15 minutes. Drain well and transfer to a bowl.

- Mash the potatoes until smooth and set the bowl aside.

- Mix in the tablespoon of soup mix, corn flour, and cheese with clean hands.

- Transfer the potato mixture to a freezer-safe sealable plastic bag. Flatten the mixture with your fingers and spread it to the edges. Seal the bag and freeze for an hour.

- After an hour, cut the bag away from the potato mix using scissors.

- Place potato mixture onto a cutting board and cut into 2.5cm-thick slices, cutting each slice in half crossways.

- Place half the potato sticks in an air fryer basket and spray the tops with oil. Turn over the sticks and spray again.

- Cook until crisp and golden, for about 10 minutes at 356°F.

- Once done, do the same with the second batch of potato sticks.

- In the meantime, combine the remaining soup mix and sour cream in a small-sized bowl. Add a tablespoon or two of water if it's too thick.

- Place the sour cream mixture in the center of a serving platter and arrange the potato sticks around it.

- Finish off with a sprinkle of sea salt flakes and chives.

Hash Brown Ham and Cheese Sandwich

Serves: 1 / Preparation time: 5 minutes / Cooking time: 5 minutes

2 cooked hash browns

20g sliced ham, coarsely chopped

1/4 cup pre-grated pizza cheese

2 teaspoons pizza sauce

- Sprinkle the sandwich press with a tablespoon of cheese into an oval shape exactly of the same size as hash brown.

- Place hash brown onto the cheese, followed by pizza sauce, ham, and a tablespoon of remaining cheese.

- Top with another hash brown, followed by a sprinkle of remaining cheese.

- Cook until the cheese has melted, for about a minute.

- Enjoy delicious hash brown ham and cheese sandwich.

10-Minute French Onion Chicken Rice Bake

Serves: 4 / Preparation time: 5 minutes / Cooking time: 5 minutes

2 x 200g tub French onion dip

1 cup coarsely grated cheddar

30g butter

1 cup coarsely grated mozzarella

200g button mushrooms, thinly sliced

450g pkt microwave basmati rice, warmed

3 green shallots, finely chopped

1 barbecue chicken, skin and bones removed, meat shredded

120g baby spinach

1/2 cup pouring cream

- Preheat butter in a skillet.

- Add three-quarters of the shallot and mushroom and sauté until softened, for 2 minutes.

- Next, stir in the spinach until wilted.

- Add cream, dip, and chicken, and bring to a simmer.

- Then simmer the mixture to your liking.

- Preheat the grill.

- Spoon rice into a baking dish (6 cups) and top with chicken mixture, followed by cheddar and mozzarella.

- Grill until the cheese has melted, for a few minutes.

- Garnish with remaining shallots, and enjoy!

Hassel bacon Potato Bake

Serves: 6 / Preparation time: 35 minutes / Cooking time: 1 hour 30 minutes

40g pkt French onion soup mix

2 tablespoons chopped fresh chives

1 1/2 cups pouring cream

2 rindless middle bacon rashers, finely chopped

3 garlic cloves

2/3 cup coarsely grated cheddar

3 fresh thyme sprigs, plus extra leaves, to serve

6 white-skinned potatoes, unpeeled, halved lengthways

- Preheat the oven to392°F.

- Cook garlic, cream, and thyme in a small-sized pan for a couple of minutes. Turn off the flame and season to your liking.

- In the meantime, place one-half potato on a chopping board (cut side down).

- Now place a bamboo skewer on each side and make thin cuts using a sharp knife, making sure not to cut all the way through.

- Do the same with the remaining potato halves.

- Place potatoes in a roasting pan, flat-side down.

- Sprinkle the top with half the bacon and half the cheese.

- Strain the prepared cream mixture into a jug through a fine sieve, discarding solids.

- Add soup mix to the cream mixture and whisk well.

- Top potatoes with the cream mixture and cover the pan with the foil tightly.

- Bake in a preheated oven until potatoes are tender, for about 40 minutes.

- Remove the cover and sprinkle the potatoes with leftover bacon and cheese.

- Bake until potatoes are tender, for half an hour.

- Finish off with a sprinkle of chives and serve right away!

Choc Mint Dessert Lasagna

Serves: 8 / Preparation time: 20 minutes / Cooking time: 2 hours 30 minutes

1/2 cup icing sugar mixture

600ml thickened cream

350g pkt Sara Lee frozen chocolate cake

Green liquid food coloring, to tint

250g pkt cream cheese, chopped, at room temperature

1 1/2 teaspoons peppermint essence

Servings:

Mint Aero chocolate, coarsely chopped

Spearmint leaves to serve, plus extra sliced

Darrell Lea Minty Crunchy Chocolate Balls, coarsely chopped

- Trim the icing from the cake using a large serrated knife. Reserve it.

- Cut the cake in half (horizontally).

- Place two cake halves in a rectangular baking dish (16 x 24cm).

- Chop the reserved icing and scatter it over the cake.

- Beat icing sugar, cream cheese, 10-12 drops food coloring, and peppermint essence in a bowl until smooth.

- Beat half the cream in a clean bowl using electric beaters until firm peaks form.

- Fold one-third of the whipped cream into the cream cheese mixture using a large metal spoon until incorporated.

- Do the same with the remaining whipped cream.

- Spread the top of the cake with the cream cheese mixture and place in the fridge until chilled, for 2 hours.

- Beat the remaining cream in a bowl using electric beaters until soft peaks form.

- Spread over the mint layer and put in the fridge for half an hour.

- Sprinkle with the chocolate balls, chopped mint aero, and spearmint leaves.

Fast and Easy Dinners

Green Goddess Salad

Serves: 5-6 / Preparation time: 5 minutes / Cooking time: 0 minutes

For The Dressing:

2 scallions, roughly chopped

Freshly ground black pepper

Juice of 2 lemons

Kosher salt

1/4 cup extra-virgin olive oil

1 teaspoon dried oregano

1/4 cup tahini

1/4 cup nutritional yeast

2 tablespoons red wine vinegar

1/2 cup fresh dill

2 cloves garlic, peeled and roughly chopped

2 small shallot, peeled and roughly chopped

1 cup baby spinach

For The Salad:

4 oz. feta (vegan or regular), crumbled

Pita chips or toasted pita for serving

1 small green cabbage, diced

Toasted sesame seeds, for garnish

2 Persian cucumbers, diced

3 scallions, thinly sliced

Fresh dill for garnish

- Add all the dressing ingredients to a blender and blitz to combine until smooth. Adjust the pepper and salt to your liking.

- Combine salad ingredients in a large-sized bowl and toss with the dressing until evenly coated.

- Serve garnished with sesame seeds and dill.

- Enjoy with pita, if desired.

Kale Cobb Salad

Serves: 4 / Preparation time: 15 minutes / Cooking time: 10 minutes

For The Miso Vinaigrette:

1/3 cup nutritional yeast

1/3 cup extra-virgin olive oil

1/4 cup red wine vinegar

1/3 cup extra-virgin olive oil

1 tablespoon dried oregano

2 cloves garlic, grated or minced

1/2 teaspoon kosher salt

3 tablespoons white miso

1 teaspoon garlic powder

Juice of 2 lemons

3 tablespoons white miso

For The Crispy Shallots:

1/4 cup all-purpose flour

2 tablespoons avocado oil

2 shallots, halved and thinly sliced

Freshly ground black pepper

Kosher salt

For The Salad:

1 cup fresh mozzarella, diced

1 1/2 cups cooked chicken breast, diced

1 head green kale, destemmed and sliced into fine ribbons

1 bunch of scallions, sliced

1 avocado, diced

1 pt. Cherry tomatoes, halved

- Combine all the miso vinaigrette ingredients in a bowl until emulsified.

- To make the crispy shallots, toss shallots with the flour until coated on all sides. Season the shallots with pepper and salt.

- Preheat avocado oil in a skillet and fry shallots for 7 to 8 minutes, until crispy and caramelized.

- To make the salad, toss all the salad ingredients with the desired amount of vinaigrette.

- Serve topped with fried shallots.

Campfire Queso

Serves: 8 / Preparation time: 5 minutes / Cooking time: 10 minutes

1/2 cup beer (such as pale ale)

1/2 (10-oz.) can Rotel tomatoes

1/2 lb. hot Italian sausage

2 cups shredded pepper jack

16 oz. Velveeta, cut into 1" cubes

Servings:

Freshly chopped cilantro

Tortilla chips

Sliced jalapeño

- Cook sausage in a cast-iron skillet over a campfire, breaking it up until no longer pink, for about 5 minutes.

- Pour beer into the skillet and deglaze it.

- Turn the heat down and stir in the pepper jack, Velveeta, and Rotel until combined.

- Serve garnished with jalapeno and cilantro, and enjoy with tortilla chips.

Bell Pepper Tuna Melts

Serves: 6 / Preparation time: 15 minutes / Cooking time: 30 minutes

1/2 small red onion, minced

4 yellow and orange bell peppers, cut into half lengthwise (seeds removed)

8 slices Swiss cheese

2 tablespoons extra-virgin olive oil

Kosher salt

1 tablespoon fresh lemon juice

Freshly ground black pepper

1 tablespoon Dijon mustard

2 (5-oz.) cans tuna, drained

2 tablespoons pickle relish

1 large stalk of celery, finely chopped

2 tablespoons chopped dill, plus more for garnish

1/3 cup mayonnaise

Freshly chopped chives for serving

- Preheat the oven to 425°F.

- Arrange pepper halves onto a baking sheet, drizzle with oil, and then season with the pepper and salt to your liking.

- Roast the peppers (cut side up) until tender, for about 20 minutes.

- In the meantime, combine Dijon, tuna, pickle relish, mayo, lemon juice, red onion, celery, and dill in a large bowl. Season the filling with pepper and salt.

- Stuff roasted peppers with the tuna mixture, followed by cheese on top.

- Broil for about 3 minutes, until cheese is bubbly.

- Serve sprinkled with chives, and enjoy!

Baked Boursin Pasta

Serves: 6 / Preparation time: 8 minutes / Cooking time: 30 minutes

20 oz. cherry tomatoes

½ teaspoon red pepper flakes

1 lb. Cavatappi pasta

½ teaspoon ground black pepper

2 (5.2 oz.) boxes Boursin Garlic and Fine Herbs Cheese

1 teaspoon kosher salt

1 ½ tablespoon olive oil

Optional topping - chopped fresh basil, chives, or parsley

- Preheat the oven to 400 °F.

- Prepare the pasta as per the directions mentioned in the package.

- Place tomatoes and Boursin in a baking dish (9x9).

- Season with salt, red pepper flakes, and pepper, and drizzle with oil.

- Bake in a preheated oven for half an hour.

- Stir the tomatoes and cheese together.

- Drain the pasta and add to the baking dish. Toss well.

- Garnish with fresh herbs and enjoy!

Spinach Pici Pasta

Serves: 2 / Preparation time: 10 minutes / Cooking time: 35 minutes

Ingredients for Spinach Pici Pasta:

1 cup of flour

Pinch of salt

1 (approx. 114 grams) box of spinach

⅓ cup olive oil

Ingredients for Garlic Butter Sauce:

½ cup pasta water

Parmesan cheese

4 clove garlic, minced

Red pepper flakes

3 tablespoons butter

Pepper

Salt

- Pulse spinach and flour in a blender or food processor until spinach is broken down.

- Slowly add in the olive oil while running the processor.

- Once the dough begins to stick, stop processing it further.

- Divide dough into gumball-sized pieces and roll into spaghetti pieces.

- Add pasta to boiling salted water and cook for 1 and a half minutes. Once it begins to float on top of the pot, add it to the sauce of your choice and enjoy!

To Make Garlic Butter Sauce:

- Preheat butter in a skillet and sauté minced garlic.

- Add pasta water (1/4 cup at a time) to the skillet.

- Add red pepper flakes, pepper, and salt to your liking.

- Next, add spinach pici pasta to the pan and toss well.

- Transfer it to a serving platter and garnish with grated Parmesan before serving.

Baked Feta Pasta

Serves: 4 to 5 / Preparation time: 5 minutes / Cooking time: 45 minutes

3 tablespoons basil, freshly chopped

2 cups cherry tomatoes

3 cups penne or fusilli, cooked

1 tablespoon Italian seasoning

1 tablespoon olive oil

1 teaspoon dried red chilli flakes

1 block feta cheese

A few pinches of ground black pepper

1 tablespoon olive oil

- Preheat the oven to 400 °F.

- Add dried chili flakes, cherry tomatoes, 1 tablespoon of olive oil, ground black pepper, and Italian seasoning to an ovenproof baking dish. Toss well.

- Place feta at the top center, followed by a drizzle of olive oil.

- Bake in a preheated oven for 45 minutes.

- Meanwhile, cook pasta as per the instructions mentioned in the package until al dente. Drain the pasta, reserving ¼ of the cooking liquid.

- Remove the dish from the oven and combine the tomatoes and feta cheese.

- Add cooked pasta and toss well.

- Add in the reserved pasta water and toss again.

- Finish off with a garnish of fresh basil.

- Enjoy warm!

Emily Mariko's Salmon Rice

Serves: 1 / Preparation time: 5 minutes / Cooking time: 0 minutes

Sriracha

Kimchi (optional)

White rice, cooked

Half an avocado (optional)

Salmon fillet, cooked

Roasted seaweed

Soy sauce

Kewpie mayo

- Start the recipe by gently flipping the salmon fillet and then spreading it across the plate.

- Top the fillet with a serving of ice, followed by Sriracha, soy sauce, and Kewpie mayo.

- Combine all the ingredients.

- Place kimchi, sliced avocado, and any other sides in a bowl.

- Wrap a chopstick full of rice with roasted seaweed and serve immediately!

Crispy Sesame Chicken

Serves: 4 / Preparation time: 2 hours / Cooking time: 20 minutes

Sesame Chicken:

Sesame seeds and dry chives optional for serving

½ teaspoon salt

1½ lbs. boneless, skinless chicken thighs cubed

White rice cooked

3 tablespoons soy sauce

Vegetable oil for frying

1 egg white

2 tablespoons cornstarch plus more on the side for additional coating

1 tablespoon minced garlic

¼ teaspoon black pepper

Honey Soy Sauce:

5 tablespoons soy sauce

1 tablespoons cornstarch dissolved in 2 tablespoons cold water

4 tablespoons honey

2 tablespoons apple cider vinegar

3 tablespoons brown sugar

4 tablespoons ketchup

4 tablespoons water

- Combine all the sesame chicken ingredients in a large-sized bowl until the chicken is evenly coated. Refrigerate for an hour or two, covered.

- Remove chicken from refrigerator and coat in dry cornstarch.

- Preheat oil in a skillet and fry chicken until evenly cooked.

- Once done, remove to a plate lined with a paper towel.

- To make sesame chicken extra crispy, fry it again and drain it on paper towels.

- Add all the sauce ingredients to a separate skillet except for the cornstarch slurry, stirring frequently.

- Once heated, stir in the cornstarch slurry until thickened.

- Turn the heat down and add cooked chicken. Toss well.

- Finish off with a sprinkle of chives, sesame seeds, and sliced green onions.

- Enjoy this delicious meal with cooked white rice!

Oyster Mushroom Fried Chicken

Serves: 5 / Preparation time: 15 minutes / Cooking time: 3 minutes

Vegetable oil for frying

Dry Mix:

½ teaspoon dried oregano

1 teaspoon MSG or 1 teaspoon sea salt

½ cup unbleached all-purpose flour

1 tablespoon white pepper

½ cup cornstarch

½ tablespoon ground ginger

1 cup panko bread crumbs

1 tablespoon garlic powder

1 teaspoon dried thyme

2 tablespoons paprika

1 teaspoon dried basil

½ tablespoon dry mustard powder

½ teaspoon black pepper

Wet Batter:

1 teaspoon celery salt

8-10 large oyster mushroom clusters

1 cup unbleached all-purpose flour

1½ cup water

¼ cup cornstarch

Optional Dips:

3 tablespoons mayo mixed with 1 tablespoon sambal oelek

Kewpie mayo

Vegan hot honey

Chick-fil-a sauce

- Preheat oil in a deep pan.

- Place a wire lack in a lipped baking sheet and do the same with another rack.

- Whisk together all the dry ingredients in a medium-sized bowl.

- Combine wet ingredients in another bowl except for mushroom oysters.

- Once the oil is hot, dip the oyster mushroom, one at a time, first into the wet batter, and then coat with a dry mixture.

- Lay mushrooms onto the wire rack and place them into the hot oil with the help of tongs. Fry the mushrooms until golden and crispy, for a couple of minutes.

- Once done, place fried mushrooms onto a clean wire cooling rack and let the excess oil drip off.

- Serve as is or with your favorite dipping sauces.

Vegan Korean Corn Cheese Ram

Serves: 2 / Preparation time: 4 minutes / Cooking time: 6 minutes

2 cups corn kernels (fresh or frozen)

1½ cup vegan cheese of choice

2 packets of ramen noodles

2 tablespoons mayonnaise

1 tablespoon butter

1 tablespoon white sugar

2 green onion, light and dark parts separated

- Add dried ramen noodles to a bowl with hot water and let them sit for a couple of minutes.

- In the meantime, preheat the butter in a pan.

- Add light parts of green onion, corn, sugar, and mayonnaise and sauté for a minute or two, stirring frequently.

- Add softened noodles along with ¼ cup of ramen water and cook for a few minutes, covered.

- Next, add ¼ cup vegan cheese and green onion and toss well.

- Serve garnished with additional green onion and vegan cheese!

Marry Me Chicken

Serves: 8 / Preparation time: 15 minutes / Cooking time: 30 minutes

Skillet Fried Chicken Breasts:

1 teaspoon garlic powder

2 tablespoons butter

2 lbs. chicken breasts pounded or sliced thin or chicken cutlets

1 teaspoon black pepper

½ cup all-purpose flour

1 teaspoon paprika

2 tablespoons vegetable oil

1 teaspoon salt

Parmesan Cream Sauce:

⅓ cup chopped sun-dried tomatoes

Red pepper flakes to taste/optional

2 tablespoons minced garlic

1 teaspoon dried thyme

1 cup chicken broth

1 teaspoon dried Oregano

1 cup heavy whipping cream

1 cup Parmesan Cheese Shredded (not grated)

Extra Marry Me Chicken Ingredients:

16 oz. Rotini Pasta cooked

½ cup shredded Parmesan Cheese for topping

1 chopped fresh parsley for topping

- Cook Rotini Pasta as per the directions mentioned in the package.

  Fry Chicken:

- Combine garlic powder, flour, black ground pepper, paprika, and salt in a small-sized bowl.

- Dredge chicken breast pieces into the flour mixture until coated on all sides.

- Preheat butter and vegetable oil in a skillet over medium flame.

- Add chicken and cook until crispy, for about 8 to 10 minutes.

- The cooking time may vary depending on the thickness of the breast piece.

- The internal temperature of the chicken should be 165.

Make Parmesan Cream Sauce:

- Combine all the parmesan cream sauce ingredients in a skillet and cook until hot and bubbly, stirring frequently.

- Turn the heat down and add cooked chicken to the cream mixture. Toss well.

Assemble Marry Me Chicken:

- Serve delicious Marry Me chicken & sauce over cooked pasta.

- Garnish with fresh parsley and remaining Parmesan, if desired.

Million Dollar Spaghetti

Serves: 8 / Preparation time: 20 minutes / Cooking time: 25 minutes

1 cup cottage cheese

2 cups shredded mozzarella cheese

1 lb. Italian sausage or ground beef

2 cups shredded cheddar cheese

24 oz. pasta sauce

½ cup sour cream

16 oz. spaghetti noodles cooked, drained, and cooled

8 oz. cream cheese brick

½ cup sour cream

- Add meat to a skillet and cook well until browned. Then remove excess grease using a paper towel and mix with a jar of pasta sauce.

- Preheat the oven to 350 °F and grease a baking dish (9×13).

- Add cooked spaghetti pasta noodles to a large baking dish along with cream cheese, cottage cheese, sour cream, and half the meat sauce. Toss well.

- Gently fold in a cup of each mozzarella and cheddar cheese.

- Pour the remaining meat sauce over the creamy noodles.

- Sprinkle with the remaining shredded cheese.

- Bake in a preheated oven for about 20 to 25 minutes.

- Once done, take it out of the oven and let it sit for a couple of minutes before serving.

Cucumber Shrimp Boats

Serves: 8 cucumber boats / Preparation time: 5 minutes / Cooking time: 10 minutes

24-pack baby shrimp	1 teaspoon furikake
Mayonnaise and Sriracha to taste	**Optional Garnishes:**
2 cucumbers, ends chopped off	Sesame seeds
1/2 teaspoon sesame oil	Chopped scallions
1 cup cooked white rice	Furikake

- Slice each cucumber in half lengthwise and crosswise. Remove the seeds and pat them dry using a clean paper towel.

- Stuff each cucumber boat with rice.

- Season the shrimp and toss with oil on all sides.

- Place shrimp in an air fryer basket and cook at 400°F for 10 minutes.

- Once done, top each cucumber boat with cooked shrimp.

- Combine mayonnaise and Sriracha and drizzle it over the shrimp.

- Top with sesame seeds, scallions, furikake, or toppings of your choice!

Tik Tok Shrimp Rice Bowl

Serves: 2 / Preparation time: 10 minutes / Cooking time: 30 minutes

2/3 lb. shrimp, peeled + deveined

2 cups sushi rice, cooked

Japanese cucumber salad:

1 tablespoon sesame oil

2 tablespoons sesame seeds

1 large cucumber, sliced thin

Salt to taste

2 tablespoons rice vinegar

1 tablespoon sugar

Assembly:

Low sodium soy sauce, to taste

Nori paper, cut into squares

1 avocado, sliced

Kewpie mayo, to taste

2 scallions, chopped

Sriracha, to taste

Shrimp:

- Place shrimp in a pot and cover with cold water. Bring it to a boil and then cook for 2 minutes. Turn off the flame and transfer to a bowl with ice and cold water. Let it sit for 5 minutes, and then chop it up.

Cucumber Salad:

- Toss cucumber with sugar, vinegar oil, salt, and oil.

- Place sesame seeds in a pan and toast them over medium-high heat.

- Once lightly toasted, transfer to a bowl with cucumber and mix well.

Assembly:

- Place shrimp in a serving platter, followed by a drizzle of Sriracha, soy sauce, and kewpie mayo.

- Top with scallions and toss well.

- Then top with salad and avocado.

- Scoop up with nori squares and eat just like sushi.

TikTok Cafeteria Noodles Recipe

Serves: 6 / Preparation time: 5 minutes / Cooking time: 15 minutes

1 tablespoon is better than a bouillon chicken base

Freshly cracked black pepper to taste

1 16 oz. bag elbow noodles

1 stick softened butter

6 1/2 cups chicken broth

2 10.5 oz. Cans cream of chicken soup

- Add bouillon and four cups of chicken broth to a pot and bring to a boil.

- Add remaining broth and noodles and stir a bit.

- Stir in the cans of condensed soup and bring to a boil. Let it cook for 2 minutes, and then turn off the flame.

- Stir in the stick of butter and cover the pot.

- Let the noodles sit for 15 to 20 minutes, stirring a few times in between.

- Season the noodles with cracked black pepper to your liking.

- Transfer to serving bowls and enjoy!

Lemon-Dijon Chicken and Rice

Serves: 4 / Preparation time: 15 minutes / Cooking time: 30 minutes

Marinade:

2 tablespoons Dijon Mustard

1 lemon juiced

2 tablespoons minced garlic

2 lemons zested on the skin

2 tablespoons vegetable oil

Chicken & Rice Bake:

3 cups water or chicken broth

Lemon slices garnish

4 chicken thighs not frozen

Paprika

1½ cups white rice

Salt and black pepper

- Add mustard, garlic, lemon zest, vegetable oil, and lemon juice to an ovenproof skillet and whisk well.

- Add in the chicken thighs and toss well until coated on all sides.

- Remove chicken and refrigerate for half an hour, covered.

- Preheat the oven to 350°F.

- Add water and rice to the same ovenproof skillet and whisk again.

- Take marinated chicken out of the freezer and add to the skillet.

- Season the chicken with pepper, salt, and paprika.

- Bake in a preheated oven for half an hour or until the chicken is cooked through.

- The cooking time may vary depending on the thickness of the chicken and the rice type.

- The internal temperature of the chicken should be 165 degrees.

- Place lemon slices in a skillet and let them be charred tightly.

- Finish off with a garnish of lemon slices.

Bourbon Chicken

Serves: 4 / Preparation time: 15 minutes / Cooking time: 10 minutes

2 tablespoons vegetable oil

Fresh parsley or green onions for serving (optional)

1½ lbs. chicken breast

White rice cooked and left warm

Bourbon Chicken Sauce:

1 tablespoon bourbon whiskey

¼ cup white sugar

1 tablespoon minced garlic

¼ cup brown sugar

1 teaspoon ground ginger

¼ cup brown sugar

¼ cup soy sauce

½ cup apple cider vinegar

- Place chicken breasts in a preheated skillet and brown on both sides. Each side will take about 5 minutes. Turn off the flame and remove the chicken.

- Once cool enough to handle, slice the cooked chicken into small cubes or bite-sized pieces.

- Combine all the bourbon chicken sauce ingredients in a skillet along with the cooked chicken.

- Cook until the chicken is hot and the sauce begins to thicken.

- Top white rice with delicious bourbon chicken garnished with green onions and chopped parsley.

Honey Buttered Fried Chicken

Serves: 4 / Preparation time: 15 minutes / Cooking time: 10 minutes

½ teaspoon baking soda

Fresh parsley optional

4 boneless, skinless chicken thighs cut into 1" cubes

Vegetable oil, for frying

½ cup all-purpose flour

½ cup ice-cold water

½ cup cornstarch

Honey Butter:

2 tablespoons white sugar

2 tablespoons honey

4 tablespoons butter

2 tablespoons soy

- Preheat oil in a skillet over medium-high heat.

- Combine cornstarch, ice water, baking soda, chicken, and flour in a large-sized bowl until the chicken is coated on all sides.

- Place chicken in hot oil and fry until golden brown and crispy, each side for 8 to 10 minutes, flipping once in between. Time may vary depending on the chicken's thickness.

- Once done, remove the chicken to a plate lined with a paper towel.

- Combine honey butter ingredients in a skillet and cook until bubbly, stirring frequently. Once begins bubbling, turn off the flame.

- Add fried chicken to the honey butter and toss until coated on all sides.

- Enjoy warm!

Air Fryer Steak Bites

Serves: 3 / Preparation time: 10 minutes / Cooking time: 7 minutes

½ teaspoon dry steak seasoning

2 tablespoons minced garlic

1 lb. Sirloin cubed, cut into 1" cubes

3 tablespoons melted butter

2 tablespoons vegetable oil

¼ teaspoon black pepper

1 teaspoon Worcestershire sauce

½ teaspoon salt

½ teaspoon dry chives

- Combine all the ingredients in a large-sized bowl except for minced garlic and melted butter and toss well until steak cubes are evenly coated.

- Place steak cubes in an air fryer basket and air fry for 7 minutes at 400 °F.

- Combine minced garlic and melted butter.

- When steak cubes are done cooking, dredge them in garlic butter and enjoy hot!

Fancy Dinners

Zucchini Bolognese

Serves: 4 / Preparation time: 10 minutes / Cooking time: 4 ½ hours

1 chicken bouillon cube

Pinch red pepper flakes

1 tablespoon extra-virgin olive oil

1 cup freshly grated Parmesan, plus more for serving

1 medium white onion, chopped

Juice of 1/2 lemon

5 medium zucchini, chopped

3/4 lb. rigatoni

1/2 cup water

Freshly ground black Pepper

Kosher salt

- Preheat oil in a pot over medium-high heat.

- Add onion and sauté for about 6 minutes, until softened.

- Next, stir in the water, zucchini, and bouillon cube.

- Add Pepper and salt to your liking, turn the heat down, and put on the lid.

- Cook until zucchini is falling apart, for about 4 hours, stirring often.

- Once the sauce is almost ready, cook pasta as per the directions mentioned in the package. Drain well and add to the zucchini pot.

- Add red pepper flakes, Parmesan, and lemon juice to the pasta and toss well.

- Enjoy topped with more Parmesan.

Creamy Tomato Vodka Pasta

Serves: 6 / Preparation time: 5 minutes / Cooking time: 20 minutes

For the Pasta:

8 oz. shells of pasta

Salt

Water

Pasta Sauce:

1/4 cup parmesan cheese (plus more for serving)

 2 to 3 tablespoons olive oil

1 tablespoon butter

1 clove garlic minced

1 tablespoon butter

1 shallot minced

1/2 cup heavy cream

1 tablespoon vodka (optional)

1 teaspoon red pepper flakes (plus more for serving)

Salt and Pepper to taste

1/4 cup tomato paste

For Serving:

Chopped basil

- Cook pasta as per the directions mentioned in the package. Drain well, reserving ½ cup of the liquid.

    To Make Gigi Hadid Sauce:

- Preheat oil in a skillet and sauté shallot and garlic until fragrant.

- Add tomato paste and red pepper flakes and continue cooking for 2 minutes.

- Next, stir in the salt, vodka sauce, heavy cream, and Pepper. Turn the heat down and simmer for 13 to 15 minutes.

- Add butter and let it melt. Combine sauce and butter together.

    To Make Pasta:

- Add reserved pasta water, cooked pasta water, and Parmesan cheese to the skillet and cook until the sauce has thickened.

- Turn off the flame and sprinkle with more parmesan cheese, chopped basil, and red pepper flakes.

- Enjoy!

Bengal Barbecue Chicken Skewers

Serves: 6 / Preparation time: 2-3 hours/ Cooking time: 15 minutes

Skewers for grilling

1 1/2 lbs. raw chicken tenders or chicken breast cut into kabob-size wedges

Marinade:

1 cup brown sugar

2 tablespoons minced garlic

1 cup teriyaki sauce

3 tablespoons fresh grated ginger

1 cup soy sauce

1 tablespoon ground pepper

1 tablespoon red wine vinegar

2 bay leaves

1/2 cup sherry wine

Polynesian Sauce:

1/2 cup crushed pineapple

3 tablespoons water

4 whole cloves

1/3 cup orange juice concentrate

1 tablespoon red wine vinegar

1/2 cup soy sauce

1 cup ketchup

1/2 cup brown sugar

1/2 cup pineapple juice

- Combine all the marinade ingredients in a large-sized bowl and marinate the chicken for 3 to 3 hours.

- Mix chicken kabob marinade ingredients and marinate chicken for a few hours or overnight in the

- To make the sauce, simmer cloves in pineapple juice and vinegar for 5 to 10 minutes.

- Remove cloves and add remaining ingredients. Bring everything to a boil and cook until the sauce has thickened.

- Preheat the grill.

- Soak skewers in water and skewer raw chicken chunks onto each kabob.

- Grill until chicken is cooked through, turning occasionally. It may take 10 to 12 minutes.

- Serve delicious grilled chicken kabobs in your dinner with plenty of sauce.

TikTok Ramen

Serves: 1 / Preparation time: 10 minutes / Cooking time: 15 minutes

1/2 teaspoon red pepper flakes

Green onions sliced

1 teaspoon butter

Everything Bagel Seasoning

1 teaspoon minced garlic

3 oz. package Ramen Noodles, toss the seasoning packet

2 teaspoons soy sauce

1/4 cup brown sugar

1 egg

- Prepare noodles as per the package directions. Drain well.

- Add brown sugar, red Pepper, soy sauce, minced garlic, and butter to a skillet. Turn on the flame and cook until sugar is dissolved, stirring frequently.

- Add pasta to the sauce and toss well until coated.

- Crack an egg and mix well.

- Once the egg is cooked through, add noodles to a serving bowl and garnish with green onions and bagel seasoning.

- Enjoy immediately!

Dump & Bake Chicken Alfredo

Serves: 8 / Preparation time: 10 minutes / Cooking time: 48 minutes

1 teaspoon Italian Seasoning

2 cups shredded mozzarella cheese

16 oz. dry rotini pasta

½ teaspoon Black Pepper

32 oz. alfredo sauce

1 teaspoon chili powder

3 cups chicken broth

1 teaspoon garlic powder

2 cups cooked shredded chicken

1 teaspoon salt

- Preheat the oven to 425 °F

- Grease a baking dish (9×13) with nonstick cooking spray.

- Add alfredo sauce, pasta, cooked and shredded chicken, chicken broth, and all seasonings. Mix well.

- Cover the dish with foil and bake in a preheated oven until hot and bubbly, for about 30 to 40 minutes.

- Take the dish out of the oven and remove the foil.

- Top with mozzarella cheese and continue baking for another 5 to 8 minutes.

- Enjoy warm!

Crack Chicken Breast

Serves: 2 / Preparation time: 5 minutes / Cooking time: 6 hours

2 cups of shredded cheese

Egg noodles

1 lb. of chicken breast

Fresh green onions for topping

1/2 cup of water (or chicken stock)

Bacon topping (cooked)

8 oz. of cream cheese (cube)

1 dry ranch dressing mix

- Grease the bottom of a slow cooker with cooking spray and place the chicken inside, followed by chicken stock or water.

- Top with cheddar cheese, cream cheese, and ranch seasoning.

- Cover and cook at low for 6 hours.

- Once done, let the chicken cool at room temperature.

- Shred the chicken and stir it with the cheese.

- Cook egg noodles as per the directions mentioned in the package. Drain well and transfer to a bowl.

- Place chicken on top of noodles and garnish with green onions and bacon pieces.

- Serve immediately!

Gigi Hadid's Spicy Vodka Pasta Sauce

Serves: 2 / Preparation time: 10 minutes / Cooking time: 45 minutes

1 teaspoon paprika

1 tablespoon vodka

2 tablespoons extra virgin olive oil

1 (16 oz.) box of rotini, boiled + reserve pasta water for later use

1 small/medium onion, diced

½ cup shredded Parmesan

1 tablespoon minced garlic

1 teaspoon garlic powder

1 tablespoon tomato paste

1 tablespoon unsalted butter

½ cup whole whipping cream

1 teaspoon red pepper flakes

½ teaspoon salt, or to taste

- Cook pasta as per the instructions mentioned in the package. Drain well, reserving a cup of pasta water.

- Combine salt, paprika, garlic powder, Pepper, and red pepper flakes in a small dish.

- Preheat oil in a skillet over medium-high heat.

- Once hot, add minced garlic and diced onion and sauté for 5 to 6 minutes, until fragrant.

- Next, add in the butter, tomato paste, whole whipping cream, and vodka to a skillet. Mix well and cook until the sauce has slightly thickened.

- Turn the heat down and stir in the shredded Parmesan until melted.

- Add ½ cup of reserved pasta cooking water to thin out the consistency of the sauce while stirring continuously.

- Cook the sauce for about 5 to 6 minutes at low, stirring constantly.

- Once done, add half the boiled rotini and toss well.

- Transfer pasta to a serving platter and top with additional cheese.

- Finish off with a pinch of fresh or dried basil.

Bang Bang Chicken Breast

Serves: 4 / Preparation time: 10 minutes / Cooking time: 15 minutes

For The Chicken:

Oil

1 teaspoon garlic powder

4 chicken breasts (thin)

Green onions

2 cups buttermilk

1/2 teaspoon pepper

1 1/2 cups cornstarch

1 teaspoon salt

1 teaspoon paprika

1 teaspoon onion powder

1 teaspoon oregano

For The Sauce:

1/2 teaspoon black pepper

1 cup mayo

1 teaspoon salt

1 teaspoon paprika

1/2 cup sweet chili sauce

1 teaspoon onion powder

1/4 cup sriracha

1 teaspoon garlic powder

1 teaspoon oregano

- Combine paprika, buttermilk, garlic, oregano, salt, and onion powder.

- Add chicken and toss well until coated on all sides. Cover the bowl and refrigerate for at least 4 hours.

- Preheat oil in a skillet.

- Combine oregano, cornstarch, salt, paprika, onion powder, Pepper, and garlic in a separate bowl.

- Place chicken breast in the cornstarch mixture and toss until coated on all sides.

- Then put in the oil and cook each side for 5 to 6 minutes, until cooked through.

- Once done, remove to a plate lined with a paper towel.

- Combine sriracha, mayonnaise, and sweet chili and pour over the chicken.

- Serve garnished with green onions, and enjoy!

Creamy Tomato and Spinach Pasta

Serves: 4 / Preparation time: 5 minutes / Cooking time: 20 minutes

4 oz. fresh spinach

1/2 lb. penne pasta

1/4 cup grated Parmesan

1 yellow onion

2 oz. cream cheese

2 cloves garlic

1/2 teaspoon dried basil

2 tablespoon tomato paste

1 tablespoon olive oil

Freshly cracked black Pepper to taste

1 15oz. can diced tomatoes

1/2 teaspoon salt

1/2 teaspoon dried oregano

1 pinch crushed red pepper (optional)

- Cook pasta as per the directions mentioned in the package. Drain well.

- In the meantime, make creamy tomato sauce. Preheat oil in a skillet and sauté minced garlic and diced onion and sauté for 3 to 5 minutes, stirring constantly.

- Next, stir in the oregano, diced tomatoes (with juices), crushed red Pepper, basil, some freshly cracked pepper, and salt.

- Add ½ cup of water and tomato sauce to a skillet and stir well for a minute or two.

- Reduce the heat and add cream cheese squares to the skillet.

- Cook until the cream has fully melted.

- Stir in the fresh spinach for a few minutes, and then add pasta. Toss well and adjust the seasonings to your liking.

- Enjoy warm!

Italian Chicken Breast

Serves: 3 / Preparation time: 5 minutes / Cooking time: 10 minutes

1 cup of Italian breadcrumbs

1 teaspoon of parsley

4 chicken cutlets (boneless breast)

1/3 cup of grated cheese (preferably Parmesan)

2 beaten eggs

- Crack eggs into a medium-sized bowl and toss well.

- Add bread crumbs, cheese, and parsley to a separate bowl and mix well.

- Dip chicken into the eggs until evenly coated on all sides, and then coat with bread crumbs.

- Preheat oil in a pan and fry chicken breast cutlets until evenly cooked.

- Once done, remove to a plate lined with a paper towel and enjoy!

Slow Cooker Olive Garden Chicken Pasta

Serves: 8 - 10 / Preparation time: 5 minutes / Cooking time: 6 hours

2 teaspoons Italian seasoning

16 oz. cooked pasta

3 chicken breasts

Salt & Pepper, to taste

1/4 cup Parmesan cheese plus more for serving

8 oz. cream cheese

16 oz. Italian Dressing

- Place chicken breast in a slow cooker and season it with Italian seasoning, Pepper, and salt.

- Pour Olive Garden Italian dressing into a slow cooker.

- Top the chicken with cream cheese and then sprinkle with parmesan cheese.

- Put the lid on and cook for 4 to 5 hours on high or 6 to 8 hours on low.

- Cook pasta as per the directions mentioned in the package.

- Shred the chicken and add pasta to a slow cooker. Toss well.

- Top with more Parmesan, and enjoy!

Crockpot Onion Soup Mix Chicken

Serves: 6 / Preparation time: 5 minutes / Cooking time: 4 hours

24 oz. bite-size potatoes cut in half

2 packets dry Lipton Onion Soup Mix

1.5 lbs. boneless, skinless chicken breast

1 cup chicken broth

30 oz. green beans canned, drained

- Place chicken breast in a slow cooker, followed by broth, one soup packet, two cans of green beans, and potatoes.

- Add another package of dry soup mix and toss lightly.

- Put on the lid and cook for 8 hours on low or 4 hours on high.

- It's ready to serve!

One-Pot French Onion Pasta

Serves: 4 / Preparation time: 10 minutes / Cooking time: 50 minutes

5 sprigs of fresh thyme

¼ cup half and half (or heavy cream or milk)

2 tablespoons butter

¼ cup parmesan cheese, freshly grated

1 large onion

1 teaspoon Worcestershire sauce

2 tablespoons sherry

3 cups beef or vegetable stock

¼ cup white wine, dry

8 oz. rigatoni uncooked

Salt and Pepper to taste

- Preheat butter in a large pot and add thinly sliced onion.

- Season the onion with a generous pinch of salt and cook for 5 minutes.

- Turn the heat down and cook until onions are caramelized, for about 20 minutes, stirring occasionally.

- Pour in the wine and sherry and deglaze the pot by scraping up the browned bits.

- Add sprigs of fresh thyme and season with Pepper and salt to your liking.

- Add rigatoni followed by Worcestershire Sauce and stock. Bring to a boil and then cook until pasta is al dente, for about 15 minutes.

- Turn off the flame and discard thyme sprigs.

- Add half and half or cream and grated parmesan cheese and stir well until combined.

- Serve right away!

TikTok's Honeycomb Pasta

Serves: 5 / Preparation time: 5 minutes / Cooking time: 45 minutes

24 oz. jar Marinara or Passata Sauce

Basil, for garnish

1 lb. Rigatoni

Water, to boil the pasta

2 tablespoons olive oil

2 tablespoons Italian Seasoning

2-3 teaspoons salt

3 cups mozzarella or cheddar cheese, shredded

- Preheat the oven to 350°F.

- Cook pasta as per the directions mentioned in the package. Once done, drain well and transfer it back to the pot.

- Sprinkle with dried Italian seasoning and drizzle with some oil. Toss well.

- Grease the bottom of the springform pan with oil and top with tomato sauce evenly.

- Line the pan with cooked pasta, followed by a sprinkle of cheese all over the rigatoni.

- Pour the remaining tomato sauce over the pasta.

- Sprinkle with the remaining cheese and bake for about 20 to 25 minutes.

- Once done, let it sit at room temperature before serving.

- Serve garnished with basil leaves.

Baked Chicken Parmesan

Serves: 4 / Preparation time: 15 minutes / Cooking time: 40 minutes

2 tablespoons grated parmesan cheese

16 oz. spaghetti noodles

24 oz. pasta sauce

Chopped fresh parsley

½ cup grated parmesan cheese

2 cups shredded mozzarella cheese

1.5 lbs. chicken breast

- Preheat the oven to 375°F.

- Spread the bottom of a baking dish (9×13) with one jar of pasta sauce.

- Add ½ cup of Parmesan and mix well.

- Next, place the chicken in a baking dish and toss it until coated with the sauce on all sides.

- Cover with foil and bake for half an hour.

- In the meantime, cook spaghetti according to the directions given in the package. Drain well, reserving a cup of the cooking water.

- Take the baking dish out of the oven and remove the foil.

- Top the chicken with mozzarella cheese, followed by 2 tablespoons of grated Parmesan.

- Transfer the dish back to the oven and continue baking for another 10 minutes.

- Toss pasta with reserve pasta water and top with the baked chicken.

- Drizzle with sauce and enjoy garnished with fresh parsley.

Chicken Cheese Cutlets

Serves: 4 / Preparation time: 8 minutes / Cooking time: 10 minutes

2 eggs beaten

1 teaspoon dried parsley

4 chicken cutlets

⅓ cup grated parmesan cheese

1 cup Italian-style breadcrumbs

- Crack eggs in a bowl and beat well.

- Combine parsley, Parmesan, and bread crumbs in a medium-sized bowl.

- Dredge chicken into beaten eggs until coated on all sides, and then coat with the crumb mixture.

- Fry in hot oil until cooked through.

- Once done, enjoy your favorite dipping.

TikTok Mexican Style Chicken, Cheese, and Rice

Serves: 4 / Preparation time: 10 minutes / Cooking time: 35 minutes

Mexican Style Rice:

16 oz. tomato sauce

1 teaspoon con de Pollo seasoning (chicken bouillon)

2 cups long-grain rice

1 teaspoon cumin

4 cups chicken broth

1 teaspoon onion powder

1 teaspoon garlic powder

Mexican Style Chicken:

Salt & pepper

1 teaspoon cumin

2-3 chicken breasts cut into bite-sized pieces

1 teaspoon garlic powder

Butter for melting

1 teaspoon onion powder

1 teaspoon dried cilantro

Queso Cheese Sauce:

1 lb. Queso Blanco Velveeta

1 tablespoon butter

1/2 cup milk

Cooking Mexican Style Rice:

- Preheat vegetable oil in a saucepan. Do not add too much oil.

- Add rice to a pan and cook until it begins to brown.

- Once it starts browning, add tomato sauce and continue cooking for another few minutes, stirring frequently.

- Next, stir in the onion powder, garlic powder, cumin, and chicken bouillon seasoning.

- Add 4 cups of chicken broth and put the lid on. Cook for 25 minutes over medium heat, stirring a few times in between.

- Once cooked, turn off the flame and let the rice sit for 10 minutes, covered.

Cooking Mexican Style Chicken:

- Add a tablespoon of butter to a skillet and let it melt.

- Add chicken breast pieces followed by all the chicken seasonings and cook over medium heat until tender.

Queso Blanco Cheese:

- Add 1 lb. of Velveeta cheese to a pan along with a tablespoon of butter and 1/2 cup of milk. Cook until the cheese has melted.

- Assemble Chicken, Cheese, and Rice:

- Transfer tomato-based rice to a serving platter and top with seasoned chicken.

- Drizzle with Queso Blanco Cheese and serve immediately!

Vegetarian Pasta with Feta Cheese

Serves: 2-3 / Preparation time: 5 minutes / Cooking time: 30 minutes

Italian herbs	1-2 cloves of garlic (pressed)
Basil	1 block feta
2 ½ cups pasta	Salt
Chili flakes (optional)	4 tablespoons olive oil
3 ⅓ cups sweet cherry tomatoes	Pepper

- Preheat the oven to 400°F.

- Place tomatoes in a baking dish and drizzle with 3 tablespoons of olive oil.

- Create space in the center and place feta block.

- Top feta block with a tablespoon of oil and sprinkle with Italian herbs, chili flakes, salt, and Pepper.

- Bake for about half an hour.

- In the meantime, prepare pasta as per the instructions given in the package. Drain well.

- After 30 minutes, take the dish out of the oven and stir in the crushed garlic until a nice creamy sauce is formed.

- Add pasta and toss well.

- Enjoy garnished with basil.

Baked Mostaccioli with Creamy Sauce

Serves: 8 / Preparation time: 15 minutes / Cooking time: 20 minutes

24 oz. pasta sauce

2 cups heavy whipping cream

Chopped Italian parsley (optional)

1 teaspoon dried oregano

16 oz. mostaccioli pasta cooked

1 tablespoon flour

2 cups shredded mozzarella cheese

1 teaspoon salt

1 lb. ground beef

½ teaspoon ground black pepper

¾ cup shredded Parmesan cheese

½ cup butter

1 teaspoon garlic powder

1 tablespoon Worcestershire sauce

- Cook the pasta as per the instructions given in the package. Drain well, reserving ½ cup of cooking liquid.
- Place beef in a skillet and season it with Pepper, garlic powder, salt, oregano, and Worcestershire sauce.
- Next, stir in the pasta sauce and turn off the flame. Set aside.
- Preheat the oven to 350°F and grease a 9×13 baking pan. Set aside.
- Combine flour and butter in a skillet and let it cook over medium flame, whisking well.
- Add shredded Parmesan and whipping cream and cook until thickened.
- Add reserved pasta water and cooked pasta, toss well, and turn off the flame.
- Transfer cheesy pasta to a prepared baking dish and top with beef mixture and 2 cups of shredded cheese.
- Bake in a preheated oven for 20 minutes.
- Serve warm sprinkled with fresh parsley!

TikTok Pizza Baguette

Serves: 6 / Preparation time: 10 minutes / Cooking time: 10 minutes

¼ cup pizza sauce

½ to ¾ cup shredded mozzarella cheese

1 Whole Baguette

¼ cup pepperoni

- Preheat the oven to 350°F.

- Slice the bread, making deep cuts every few inches. Do not cut all the way through.

- Spoon sauce into each cut until fully saturated.

- Place pepperonis in the cuts as much as you want.

- Sprinkle mozzarella over the top and bake for 8 minutes.

- Then broil for 2 minutes and enjoy immediately!

Sweet Treats

Hot Chocolate Bombs

Serves: 6 / Preparation time: 5 minutes / Cooking time: 30 minutes

1/4 cup unsweetened cocoa powder

6 cups milk, any kind

2 cups chocolate chips

Sprinkles for decorating

2 teaspoons coconut or vegetable oil

1/3 cup white chocolate chips or other assorted chocolate for drizzling

1/3 cup dry milk powder

Mini marshmallows

1/3 cup powdered sugar

- Add chocolate and oil to a microwave-safe bowl and microwave in 30-second bursts until completely melted. You'll need to stir after each burst.

- Add a few tablespoons of melted chocolate to the bottom of 12 (2.5") silicone sphere molds, spreading the chocolate to the bottom and sides using a spoon. Chill for half an hour in the freezer.

- In the meantime, prepare a hot chocolate mix by combining powdered sugar, milk powder, and cocoa powder.

- Remove frozen chocolate from the mold and fill half of each mold with hot chocolate mixture (2 tablespoons each) and a few marshmallows.

- Place a small-sized microwave-safe plate in the microwave and let it heat for just 15 seconds.

- Place one of the unfilled shells onto a warm plate so the edge will melt slightly.

- Place the filled shell on top to seal it together.

- Fill any holes or gaps with extra melted chocolate.

- Repeat the same with the remaining molds.

- Add chocolate chips to a small microwave-safe bowl and melt in 30 seconds intervals, stirring every time.

- Drizzle chocolate bombs with the melted chocolate and top with the sprinkles.

- Heat a cup of milk and pour it into a mug. Drop a chocolate bomb into hot milk and allow the chocolate to melt, and release the mix inside. Stir well.

- NOTE: a cup of milk for each bomb.

TikTok's Brown Butter Chocolate Chip Cookies

Serves: 10-12 / Preparation time: 15 minutes / Cooking time: 20 minutes

1 egg

3/4 cup dark chocolate chunks

1/2 cup unsalted butter, browned

1 1/2 cups all-purpose flour

1/2 cup granulated sugar

1 teaspoon baking soda

3/4 cup brown sugar

Splash of vanilla

- Take a cookie sheet and line it with non-wax parchment paper.

- Preheat butter in a small saucepan. Once melted, turn off the flame.

- Combine granulated sugar, brown butter, and brown sugar in a bowl until combined.

- Next, stir in the vanilla and egg until incorporated.

- Sift baking soda and flour into the mixture and start folding the ingredients together until well combined.

- Add most of the dark chocolate chunks to the dough and roll the dough balls.

- Chill dough for half an hour, covered.

- Preheat the oven to 350°F.

- Take the dough out of the fridge, scoop a tablespoon portion, and place it onto a prepared cookie tray. Do the same with the remaining dough. Make sure to evenly space the cookies.

- Roll each dough ball in reserved chocolate chunks and bake until cookies are golden brown, for about 12 to 14 minutes.

- Once done, remove them from the oven and let them cool before serving.

Oreo Sushi

Serves: 4 / Preparation time: 20 minutes / Cooking time: 0 minutes

2 tablespoons condensed milk   1 packet oreo biscuits

- Separate Oreo cream and Oreo biscuits into two bowls.

- Crush Oro biscuits in a processor until fine.

- Add 2 tablespoons of condensed milk to the fine biscuits and mix well until they are in a pliable consistency.

- Place the Oreo biscuit on parchment paper or a cling film and roll it as thin as possible using a rolling pin.

- Top with Oreo cream and spread evenly.

- Then roll it up like sushi.

- Cut it out using a sharp knife.

Apple Cider Mimosas

Serves: 1 / Preparation time: 5 minutes / Cooking time: 0 minutes

2 oz. apple cider, chilled

2 oz. Champagne or Prosecco, chilled

Cinnamon sugar

- Start by dipping a rim of the glass into water and then coating it with cinnamon sugar.

- Pour vinegar into the glass, followed by Prosecco or champagne on top.

- Serve right away!

Hot Cocoa Bombs

Serves: 6 / Preparation time: 20 minutes / Cooking time: 2 minutes

2 tablespoons Hot Cocoa Mix (per cocoa bomb)

6 oz. hot water

12 oz. chocolate candy melts or chocolate chips

Additional fillings as desired

- Place chocolate in a microwave-safe bowl and cook in the microwave for 15-30 second increments, stirring frequently.

- Once melted, pour the chocolate into each mold, coating the entire circle. You should need to coat all the shells very quickly.

- Place mold in the freezer for 5 minutes.

- Then add a second chocolate layer until the mold is completely covered.

- Place the mold back in the freezer for another 5 minutes.

- Gently pop each chocolate sheet out of the mold.

- Add 2 tablespoons of cocoa mix to one-half of each shell.

- Preheat a microwave-safe plate in the microwave for 1 and a half minutes.

- Once warm, take one empty chocolate shell and press on the plate to melt the edges slightly.

- Then place it on top of the filled chocolate shell half.

- Place one cocoa bomb in a mug, followed by 6 oz. of hot water.

- Stir and enjoy!

Boozy Pineapple Spears In Malibu Rum

Serves: 1 / Preparation time: 10 minutes / Cooking time: 0 minutes

1 large whole golden pineapple, cut off the bottom and top

½ cup pure coconut water

1 cup Malibu Rum

- Stand the pineapple on a flat surface.

- Peel off the outer skin, curving gently to preserve the flesh as much as you can.

- Trim hard parts or seeds of the skin, if any.

- Start slicing straight down the pineapple center to create two long halves. Do this again to create 4 sections in total.

- Remove the tough core from the center of each and then slice into 12 to 14 spears.

- Divide the pineapple spears between two washed and dried mason jars. If spears are not fitting in the jar, trim them a little bit.

- Whisk coconut water and Malibu in a measuring cup until well-combined and pour over the pineapple spears.

- Seals the jars with a lid and refrigerate for 3 to 4 hours.

- Serve chilled!

Creamy Lemonade

Serves: 6 / Preparation time: 8 minutes / Cooking time: 0 minutes

¼ cup granulated sugar

5 cups water

½ cup freshly squeezed lemon juice

1 lemon, sliced

¼ cup sweetened condensed milk

4 cups ice

- Combine condensed milk, lemon juice, a cup of water, and sugar in a pitcher and stir well until combined.

- Stir in the ice and remaining water.

- Serve garnished with lemon slices.

- Enjoy!

White Claw Slushie

Serves: 2 / Preparation time: 5 minutes / Cooking time: 0 minutes

1 shot vodka

2 cups ice

1 can White Claw Mango

1 cup frozen strawberries and mango

- Add all the ingredients to a blender and blitz to combine until smooth.

- Pour into glasses and serve chilled!

Kitkat Cheesecake

Serves: 16 slices / Preparation time: 30 minutes / Cooking time: 0 minutes

Base;

¼ cup butter, melted

401 g Oreos, crushed (3 packets)

Cheesecake;

½ cup icing sugar

640 g kitkat family blocks

3 cups cream cheese, room temperature

2 teaspoons vanilla extract

1 cup whipping cream (heavy cream, double cream)

Base;

- Take a 22cm round cake tin or springform pan with a loose bottom and line it with greased parchment paper. Set aside.

- Crush the Oreos and combine them with melted butter. Press this mixture into the bottom of the prepared pan and place in the fridge until needed.

- Line the sides of your cake pan or springform pan with the fingers of KitKats.

- Put it in the fridge.

Cheesecake;

- Beat the softened cream cheese in a bowl until there are no lumps.

- Stir in the vanilla extract and icing sugar until smooth.

- Beat in the cream until the mixture is slightly stiff.

- Lightly crush the KitKats into small pieces and add to the cheesecake mixture. Stir well.

- Pour this mix over the Oreo crust and spread evenly.

- Let it rest overnight or for a few hours at least.

- Decorate with KitKats before serving, and enjoy!

Deep Fried Oreos

Serves: 30 / Preparation time: 10 minutes / Cooking time: 20 minutes

1 large egg

1 (18 oz.) package of cream-filled
chocolate sandwich cookies

2 quarts vegetable oil. for frying

1 cup pancake mix

1 cup milk

2 teaspoons vegetable oil

- Preheat oil in a saucepan or a deep fryer to 375°F.

- Whisk 2 teaspoons of vegetable oil, egg, and milk in a medium-sized bowl.

- Add pancake mix and stir well until no lumps are there.

- Now start dipping cookies in the batter, one at a time.

- Place cookies in hot oil and fry for about 2 minutes, until golden brown.

- Once done, remove to a plate lined with a paper towel and serve immediately!

Watermelon Pizza

Serves: 1 / Preparation time: 10 minutes / Cooking time: 0 minutes

1/2 cup raspberries

Honey or maple syrup (optional)

1 watermelon

1/2 cup pomegranate seeds

1 cup coconut yogurt (or Greek yogurt for non-vegan)

1/2 cup blueberries

1/2 cup strawberries, sliced in half

1/2 cup cherries

- Cut off a 2 to a 3-inch slice of watermelon right down in the center.

- Spread yogurt around the watermelon evenly using a spatula, leaving a little space at the top.

- Layer the top with fresh fruit. You can add as many toppings as you want.

- Drizzle with maple syrup or honey, and serve immediately!

Oreo Mug Cake

Serves: 1 / Preparation time: 30 seconds / Cooking time: 1 minute

4 Oreos

3 tablespoons milk

Whipped cream (optional)

- Add Oreo cookies to a mug and crush them using a fork as much as you can.

- Stir in the milk, crushing the cookies until they get softened.

- Place the mug in a microwave and cook for a minute.

- If the mixture still looks liquid, cook for another 30 seconds.

- Enjoy topped with whipping cream!

Frozen Jello Grapes

Serves: 2 cups / Preparation time: 10 minutes / Cooking time: 0 minutes

2 cups grapes, stems removed   1 0.6 oz. sugar-free jello

- Wash the grapes and place them in a gallon zip-lock bag.

- Pour jello over the grapes and seal the bag.

- Shake it well until the grapes are evenly coated with jello.

- Open the bag and place it onto a cookie sheet.

- Put them in the freezer until ready to eat.

Snickers No Churn Ice Cream

Serves: 6 / Preparation time: 15 minutes / Cooking time: 0 minutes

½ cup milk

Caramel Sauce

16 oz. heavy whipping cream

3 cups Snickers Candies cut into small pieces

14 oz. sweetened condensed milk

1 teaspoon vanilla extract

- Set a cup of Snickers candies aside.

- Combine condensed milk, whipping cream, and vanilla extract in a bowl fitted with a wire whisk. Beat well for about 5 to 6 minutes until stiff peaks form.

- Gently fold in cups of candies and pour half of this mixture into a casserole dish (2-1/2 quart). Spread evenly.

- Drizzle caramel in the center and top with the leftover mixture.

- Again, drizzle with the caramel and place reserved candies on top.

- Cover the dish with plastic wrap and freeze overnight or for 4 hours at least.

- Scoop into dishes or cones before serving!

Crème Brulee With Ice Cream

Serves: 2 / Preparation time: 10 minutes / Cooking time: 35 minutes

1 egg yolk

1 cup Ice Cream

Sugar Topping:

2 tablespoons water

3 tablespoons granulated white sugar

- Preheat the oven to 325°F.

- Place ice cream in a microwave-safe bowl and microwave until just softened but not hot. Refrigerate for a few hours until hard.

- Take out from the freezer and whisk in egg yolk until incorporated.

- Divide the mixture between 2 ramekin dishes and place them in a baking pan.

- Half-fill the pan with hot water and bake in a preheated oven for 35 minutes.

- Take it out of the oven and let it cool for an hour.

- Then refrigerate again for a few hours.

- Add water and sugar to a pan just before serving and bring to a boil until the sugar crystals are dissolved. Once turned caramel color, turn off the flame and pour it on top of each ramekin.

- Refrigerate until hard, for 2 to 3 hours.

- Serve immediately!

Coconut Cloud Smoothie

Serves: 1 / Preparation time: 2 minutes / Cooking time: 3 minutes

1/4 cup pineapple frozen

Vanilla stevia or other sweetener to taste

1/4 cup coconut cream cold

1 teaspoon blue Majik spirulina plus extra

1/3 cup vanilla almond milk

1 teaspoon vanilla

1/2 avocado frozen

1 scoop vanilla collagen powder

1/2 banana frozen

2 teaspoons almond butter

- Whip the coconut cream using a frother or whisk until light and fluffy.
- Add ¼ of the whipped coconut cream to the bottom of the glass, reserving 2 tablespoons for topping.
- Sprinkle the sides of the glass with blue majik.
- Add the remaining ingredients to a blender and blitz to combine until smooth.
- Pour into the prepared glass and enjoy topped with coconut cream!

Strawberry Candy Straws

Serves: 10 straws / Preparation time: 5 minutes / Cooking time: 0 minutes

1 lime, juiced or 2 tablespoons lime juice

Tajin, to taste

5 pieces of rice paper, cut in half

1 tablespoon citric acid, as needed

2 cups fruit of choice like; mango, peaches, and berries, cut into thick rectangular slices

¼ cup + 2 tablespoons granulated white sugar

- Combine a tablespoon of citric acid and ¼ cup of granulated sugar in a small-sized bowl.

- Take another bowl and combine tajin and 2 tablespoons of granulated sugar.

- Now sprinkle both sugars onto a plate along the length of the rice paper. Keep it aside.

- Pour lime juice and warm water into a lipped plate.

- Now start soaking rice paper, one at a time, in the warm water until softened, or for 20 seconds, and then place it onto a cutting board.

- Place fruit on one end of the rice paper and roll it up tightly so it will resemble a straw.

- Now roll the rice paper in the sugar variations until coated on all sides, and serve right away!

Milk Toast

Serves: 1 / Preparation time: 5 minutes / Cooking time: 10 minutes

1 tablespoon brown sugar

Bananas for topping

2 whole bread slices

Maple syrup for topping

2 tablespoons butter

⅓ cup milk

- Spread 2 bread slices with a generous amount of butter on both sides.

- Preheat the butter and add buttered slices. Allow them to cook for a minute or two.

- Sprinkle both slices with brown sugar and place one slice over another.

- Pour milk over the slices.

- Once the bread absorbs the milk, add a little more and continue toasting until the bread turns golden color and the milk is absorbed.

- You can also apply a little butter to make your toast crispier.

- Remove to a serving platter and top with bananas or any fruit of your choice.

- Drizzle with maple syrup or honey, and enjoy!

Giant Peanut Butter Rice Cake

Serves: 1 / Preparation time: 2 minutes / Cooking time: 10 minutes

2 tablespoons dark chocolate chips

1 pinch of flaky sea salt optional; for garnishing

1 rice cake

1/2 teaspoon coconut oil

1-2 tablespoons peanut butter

- Spread peanut butter on top of the rice cake evenly.

- Add coconut oil and chocolate to a microwave-safe bowl and microwave in two 30-second increments, stirring every time.

- Drizzle melted chocolate over the peanut butter, followed by a sprinkle of flay salt.

- Place rice cake in the freezer for 10 minutes.

- Once solidified, remove it from the freezer and enjoy!

TikTok's Jam & Sparkling Water Drink

Serves: 1 / Preparation time: 5 minutes / Cooking time: 0 minutes

A squeeze of lemon (optional)

1 heaping tablespoon of your jam of choice

Ice cubes (optional)

1 can sparkling water

- Add ice to the glass, followed by a heaping spoonful of any of your favorite jams.

- Pour a can of sparkling water over the jam.

- You can replace sparkling water with a hard seltzer for a cocktail.

- Stir the jam using a straw or spoon until the jam is completely dissolved.

- Enjoy!